Always Ready, A Life of Firsts, Service and Second Acts

A Memoir

Gregory A. Duncan

Copyright ©2025
All rights reserved. Written permission must be secured from the author to reproduce any part of the book.

Printed in the United States of America

ISBN: 979-8-9908317-1-1

10 9 8 7 6 5 4 3 2 1

EMPIRE PUBLISHING
www.empirebookpublishing.com

*Disclaimer: These views are mine and should not be constructed as the views of the U.S. Coast Guard, DHS, and DoD.

INTRODUCTION

"Who is Greg Duncan?

This question has been asked many times. At age 56, Greg Duncan describes himself as 'semi-retired,' actively engaged in self-growth with a daily mission of 'paying it forward' and 'placing a smile on someone's face.' But this simple description barely scratches the surface of the man whose story unfolds in these pages.

As his mother and the author of this introduction, I have watched Greg's journey with immense pride—a journey that encompasses triumph and struggle, formal and spiritual education, and unwavering service to both country and community.

Born in Chicago and raised in Inglewood, CA, Greg's early life was a tapestry of diverse cultural influences. These experiences in the bustling urban environments of Chicago and Inglewood helped forge his unique worldview, one that has guided him through various chapters of his life. His fair skin, fiery red hair, and mischievous brown eyes may have led some to underestimate him, but those who truly know him understand the depth of his character and the strength of his convictions.

Throughout his life, Greg has faced challenges with resilience and grace. His commitment to serving others has remained steadfast, demonstrating a profound belief in the importance of giving back and making a difference. He is a man of faith, living with intention and striving to embrace each moment fully.

This memoir is not just a recounting of events; it is a testament to the extraordinary life of Greg Duncan—a life marked by love, dedication, and an unwavering spirit. As we embark on this journey together, I invite you to explore the layers that make up this remarkable man."

-.Sharon A. Duncan - Mother

Table of Contents

INTRODUCTION

Chapter 1

The Eye of The Storm 1

Chapter 2

The Genesis of An Entrepreneur 10

Chapter 3

Foundations and Formations 13

Chapter 4

Building a Life 17

Chapter 5

Navigating New Horizons 24

Chapter 6

My Professional Experience 32

Chapter 7

"The Middle"; Life Started, and "My Longest Relationship" . 37

Chapter 8

Family and Commitment 43

Chapter 9

Marriage; Another Level of Commitment 50

Chapter 10

Higher Learning: The Gift That Keeps Giving.. 53

Chapter 11

The Creativity Space; Freedom to Just Be… 56

Chapter 12

Community and Spirituality; A Place to Connect 59

Chapter 13

Forged in Fire: Finding Strength in Adversity 61

Chapter 14

Mentorship and Community Service: A Way of Life 65

Chapter 15

Lessons Learned: The Bends and Tweaks Along the Way 68

Chapter 16

Accomplishments, Celebration, Recognition; Do It! 70

Chapter 17

Relationship, Life Partner, Next Chapter in Motion 73

APPENDIX

Significant Professional Achievements and Positions 79

CHAPTER 1
THE EYE OF THE STORM

Smooth seas do not make skillful sailors.

– African Proverb

My introduction to the U.S. Coast Guard was entirely unexpected—a simple invitation that would irrevocably alter the course of my life. My boss, an enlisted reservist, extended an invitation to visit the Coast Guard station in Channel Islands, California. Lacking any military background and harboring no ambitions to join, I felt like a moth drawn to a flame—an inexplicable pull toward something unknown. Yet, something about that day resonated deeply. The sleek boats slicing through the water, the rhythmic hum of the station's operations, and the unspoken camaraderie among the crew—it all captivated me. This visit planted a seed that blossomed into a commitment to the reserves, transforming a part-time obligation into a central pillar of my life, forging my sense of discipline, purpose, and service.

Years later, having departed full-time service in the Coast Guard and settled into civilian life, the Coast Guard extended another offer—a once-in-a-lifetime opportunity. They asked me to return to active duty, transitioning from my drilling reserve status to full-time service. This wasn't just another deployment; it was a chance to reach the pinnacle of my career, a golden ticket to a world I'd only glimpsed. The decision weighed heavily, like a ship caught in a turbulent sea. It meant upending my established life, abandoning the stability I'd built, and embarking on a journey into the unknown. After lengthy discussions with my family, employer, and girlfriend—all offering unwavering support—I embraced the challenge. The siren call of the unknown was irresistible. As the pieces fell into place, an exhilarating anticipation began to build, overshadowing the daunting nature of the path ahead.

The onboarding process was a whirlwind, a maelstrom of paperwork and preparation. The initial hurdle—a nomination and security clearance check—felt like excavating the remnants of my past: years of records, a polygraph test, and expedited interviews that delved into the deepest recesses of my history. The intensity was palpable, yet I navigated it with relative ease.

By May 2020, I was fully immersed in a grueling year-long training program designed to prepare me for a role unlike any I'd ever undertaken. The training was relentless: the Joint Military Attaché School (JMAS) honed my diplomatic skills; intensive French lessons pushed me to my linguistic limits (oui, oui!); the Foreign Affairs Counter Threat (FACT) course equipped me to survive hostile environments; weapons qualifications maintained my edge; and countless consultations around Washington, D.C., consumed my days. The sheer volume of information, coupled with its rapid delivery, was overwhelming. Yet, I was humbled and honored to be selected for such a prestigious position. I knew this represented the apex of my career.

Then came the assignment that would redefine everything: Haiti—a land of breathtaking beauty, profound challenges, and a history as intricate as a finely woven tapestry. While I possessed limited knowledge of the country prior to the mission, my innate love for travel and exploration made the unknown alluring. Haiti promised an immersion into a vibrant culture, a rich experience I yearned to understand. However, I was also acutely aware of the considerable challenges: political instability, widespread poverty, and severe resource shortages were only the beginning. The "people stuff," as I termed it—the complexities of interpersonal dynamics and team management under extreme pressure—would prove equally demanding. Despite this, I was ready. My expectations were tempered, but my resolve remained unshaken.

Upon landing in Port-au-Prince on July 6, 2021, I never anticipated the immediate crisis that awaited. A late-night phone call shattered the quiet of my first night. Initially dismissing it as a prank, persistent knocking at my door revealed the grim reality. A senior military official stood there, her expression as grave as a storm cloud. "Sorry to wake you, sir... the president has been assassinated." The words struck me like a bolt of lightning. "Which president?" I stammered, still disoriented from sleep. "The Haitian president," she replied. My mind reeled. Barely six hours into my assignment, Haiti's already fragile political landscape had plunged into utter chaos. The gentle introduction I had anticipated was nowhere to be found.

If that first night felt like a baptism by fire, the ensuing weeks and months were a tempestuous storm at sea. On August 14, 2021, just over a month after my arrival, a 7.2-magnitude earthquake ravaged Haiti's southern peninsula, reducing towns to rubble and leaving thousands dead or injured. The devastation was breathtaking, a landscape scarred by loss and ruin. As if nature itself conspired against recovery, just two days later, Tropical Depression Grace swept across the shattered landscape, flooding streets and exacerbating the suffering of those who had already lost everything. Relief efforts were chaotic, resources were severely strained, and tensions ran high. There was no respite, only a relentless succession of crises that tested the limits of human endurance.

Then, on October 16, 2021, while the country was still struggling to recover, another tragedy unfolded. Seventeen American and Canadian missionaries were kidnapped by a local gang, sparking a 60-day FBI investigation. In a remarkable twist of fate, these hostages managed to escape when their captors, likely under the influence of drugs, lost their vigilance, allowing the captives to navigate their way under the stars to a nearby farm. From there, they contacted the U.S. Embassy, their ordeal a testament to both human desperation and the indomitable spirit of resilience. The relentless string of disasters—both natural and man-made—felt surreal. I had barely settled into my role when the ground beneath my feet—both literally and figuratively—began to shift.

The situation in Haiti deteriorated further. Gang activity exploded across the capital, with gangs controlling over 80% of Port-au-Prince and surrounding areas. This pervasive violence casts a long shadow of fear and instability, permeating daily life. Gasoline became a scarce and precious commodity, only intermittently available on the black market. Corruption reached unprecedented levels, elections remained elusive, and the economy was teetering on the brink of collapse. The interim government struggled to maintain even a semblance of order, like a ship adrift without a rudder in a raging storm.

The airport in Port-au-Prince, considered a "red line" by the U.S. as a vital lifeline, barely functioned. Haiti's emergency and crisis management systems were virtually nonexistent. The police and military, despite achieving small victories, were largely ineffective. Enforcement was inconsistent, unable to counter the rampant daily kidnappings for ransom—a lucrative enterprise for the gangs. Canada and the U.S. withheld military security assistance and refused to lead any security force. The persistent lack of food, education, and healthcare continued to cripple the nation. The UN engaged in endless debates with the U.S., Caribbean member countries, and others regarding the deployment of a multinational security force to reclaim control of the streets from the gangs.

Amidst this chaos, I coined the phrases "every day is Monday" and "my fun meter," using them both within my circles and beyond. I was even questioned about "every day is Monday" by the Southern Command Combatant Commander; I advised her against further inquiry (lol). Yes, I explained, every day felt like a Monday, except when Monday was a local holiday.

Haiti. The very name now evokes a whirlwind of emotions—memories etched deeply within me. Back in my twenties, Haiti was merely a distant whisper, a place I'd never considered. The challenges I'd faced then, the lessons learned in the crucible of my youth, were subtly preparing me for a future I couldn't have fathomed—a future inextricably linked to this vibrant, complex, and troubled island nation. Here is one of the many lessons I learned in Haiti.

The Weight of Command (and Leadership)

Leading such a chaotic mission in Haiti was one of the most challenging and defining experiences of my career. The mission was as multifaceted as it was urgent. With thousands of lives at stake, our task required collaboration across a spectrum of agencies (most of the 3 and 4 letter agencies)—each with its own priorities. Some were focused on intelligence gathering, others on stabilizing the region, while humanitarian organizations worked to deliver critical aid. All of this unfolded against the backdrop of a country already grappling with instability, exacerbated by gang activity and a lack of essential infrastructure.

Securing the area was paramount. Humanitarian supplies intended for earthquake victims were vulnerable to theft and corruption, often redirected to the black market. Before helicopters could land or aid could be distributed, we had to ensure the safety of those resources and the people delivering them. It was a delicate balance of diplomacy and action—coordinating with international partners, local police when they had capacity, and working with local communities while mitigating threats that could derail the operation.

At the same time, I recognized that the success of the mission depended not just on strategy but on the well-being of my team. When I arrived, many of them were burned out, having gone months without leave. Despite operating at only 60% staffing capacity, I implemented a policy requiring everyone to take time off. It wasn't optional; it was essential.

They needed to step away, decompress, and reconnect with themselves so they could return ready to face the relentless demands of the mission. I insisted on leading by example, ensuring I was the last to take leave, but I never let anyone compromise their health for the sake of the operation.

Navigating this environment required direct, honest communication, even when it ruffled feathers among senior leaders. I frequently found myself in tense conversations with high-ranking officials who underestimated the gravity of the situation on the ground. My role demanded that I speak truth to power—advocating for my team and the mission's needs, no matter how uncomfortable those discussions became. It wasn't always well-received at the moment, but later, many of those same leaders expressed their respect for the work we accomplished and the clarity I brought to the table.

This mission was a stark reminder of the dual realities we face in leadership. On one side, there was the weight of coordinating life-saving operations in a chaotic and dangerous environment. On the other hand, there were the personal sacrifices—being away from family, missing milestones, and knowing that those you care about were carrying their own burdens in your absence. It's a balance I've struggled with throughout my career, but Haiti taught me that leadership isn't just about solving problems; it's about showing up for your team and for the people who depend on you, no matter how impossible the circumstances may seem.

Haiti tested me in ways I could never have predicted. The weight of the crises, the constant urgency, and the relentless pressure for solutions pushed me to my limits—but they also revealed something profound: the extent of my resilience, my capacity for adaptation, and my potential to lead in the face of unimaginable chaos. This memoir is my attempt to capture those moments—the triumphs and heartbreaks, the lessons learned, and the transformation they wrought within me.

Chapter 2
THE GENESIS OF AN ENTREPRENEUR

A mentor is someone who allows you to see the hope inside yourself.

– Oprah Winfrey

From a young age, I was drawn to the hustle—a relentless drive to carve out my own path. The crisp morning air felt invigorating against my skin as I slung a heavy bag of newspapers over my shoulder, each step a testament to my determination not to rely on anyone else. At twelve, I wasn't just delivering papers; I was sowing the seeds of independence in the fertile soil of my neighborhood. The rhythmic rustle of the pages and the occasional bark of a neighborhood dog became the soundtrack of my mornings, a symphony heralding the dawn of my early entrepreneurial spirit.

This drive to succeed on my own terms followed me into my twenties, like the persistent beat of a drum. While my peers often pursued the same old diversions—sometimes wandering into the thickets of poor choices—I sought different influences. I intentionally surrounded myself with an older crowd—people whose experiences and wisdom far surpassed the typical folly of youth. They weren't just older; they were life mentors who opened their world to me, a realm where conversations were rich with lessons on life and business. I soaked up their wisdom like a sponge, grateful for the clarity it brought to my decision-making. It was a turning point, a revelatory moment realizing how crucial one's environment is to personal growth.

Guided by this newfound wisdom, an older friend—an embodiment of experience—pulled me aside one day. "You won't get ahead unless you're the one signing the checks," he imparted in a hushed tone, a piece of advice that ignited a fire within me. It was a spark that illuminated the path toward my ambitions.

Spurred by that insight, I founded Duncan Security Consultants, Inc. The company was my brainchild, a tangible manifestation of my dreams that took flight with astonishing speed, ballooning to over 300 employees. Yet, just as a storm can rise unexpectedly, the events of 9/11 shattered the mundane. Duty called me back to the U.S. Coast Guard, and I found myself torn between my burgeoning business and a higher call to service. I made the heart-wrenching decision to sell my shares, stepping away from the company I had nurtured like a gardener tending to a precious sapling.

The transition was anything but smooth. Although my departure left the company in capable hands—my mother and a few trusted managers—it was over-leveraged by a loan I had personally guaranteed. The weight of this financial burden pressed heavily on my shoulders, like an anchor dragging me down, culminating in the closure of the company and a personal financial loss. It was a humbling lesson in risk and resilience—one that taught me the harsh realities of entrepreneurship. Through this trial, I learned that failure is not the end; it is merely a stepping stone in the relentless pursuit of growth.

As I reflect on these experiences, I appreciate the diverse tapestry of learning environments that shaped me. Whether in the structured confines of a classroom, the unpredictable streets filled with possibility, or the wisdom-filled gatherings with my older friends, each setting offered unique lessons. In a dojo, I learned the art of discipline and focus; in boardrooms, the intricacies of negotiation and leadership. These varied experiences honed my senses, transforming me into a lifelong learner—a seeker of knowledge who thrives on new challenges.

Yet, standing on the cusp of the future, I am acutely aware of the rapid changes sweeping through society. Information—often unverified—floods our consciousness, and I've observed a concerning trend towards complacency. The diligence of old-school research and critical thinking is often overshadowed by the allure of instant gratification. It's a shift that worries me, yet one I believe can be countered by a return to thoughtful inquiry.

In navigating this era of change, I hold fast to the values instilled in me by my upbringing. Raised as a mixed-race individual, I celebrate differences and embrace diversity, refusing to be confined by societal labels. This perspective shapes my vision for the future—a future where unity and respect for diverse perspectives can overcome division and discord. My simple take is that the country needs a foundation based on true equality, where every individual is respected and celebrated for their unique contributions.

As I close this chapter, I carry these lessons forward. Life is a complex tapestry, best navigated by simplifying the intricate and embracing the unknown. The journey continues, and I remain committed to learning, growing, and adapting—ever ready for the challenges and opportunities that lie ahead.

CHAPTER 3
FOUNDATIONS AND FORMATIONS

We carry within us the wonders we seek around us.

– Sir Thomas Browne

Birth to a New Beginning (Ages 0-10)

In April 1967, my entry into the world came at a time rife with monumental historical events that profoundly shaped the era. The decade vibrated with the echoes of Yuri Gagarin's pioneering orbit around the Earth, igniting a global fascination with space and the bold possibilities beyond our atmosphere. America was still reeling from the assassination of President John F. Kennedy, a national trauma that reshaped American politics and left a lingering shadow of what-ifs over the nation.

It was also a period marked by Dr. Martin Luther King Jr.'s stirring "I Have a Dream" speech delivered on the steps of the Lincoln Memorial—a clarion call for equality and justice, resonating powerfully even as his life would tragically be cut short. The glamorous yet troubled life of Marilyn Monroe had recently ended, her legacy a complex tapestry woven into the cultural and political fabric of the time. Meanwhile, Muhammad Ali, known as the world's heavyweight champion, stood as a symbol of resilience and defiance that transcended the confines of boxing.

Amid these significant societal shifts, the scientific community celebrated a groundbreaking achievement with the first successful human heart transplant, heralding a new age of medical innovation and expanding hope for humanity's ability to overcome its physical limitations.

My early childhood, set against this backdrop of profound change and innovation, began in Chicago, Illinois. In 1970, amidst these transformative times, my family made the significant decision to relocate to Inglewood, California. This move marked not just a change in geography but a leap into a new life filled with the promise of sunshine and fresh opportunities.

These formative years were a vivid juxtaposition of global upheavals and personal adventures. As a child, my worldview was profoundly influenced by the echoes of these events and shaped by the direct experiences of family road trips in my father's vintage Volkswagen bus. He often took on the roles of both chauffeur and entertainer, infusing our journeys with laughter and light-heartedness, which contrasted starkly with the complexity of my parents' relationship. My mother, ever the nurturing force, worked tirelessly to create a home environment that radiated warmth and stability amidst the external chaos.

These early experiences laid a complex foundation for understanding personal identity against the backdrop of a world in relentless flux. They instilled in me lessons about the resilience required to navigate life's uncertainties and the power of hope and ambition that were so characteristic of the era into which I was born.

The Formative Years (Ages 11-15)

As adolescence took hold, my entrepreneurial spirit began to awaken. Life in Inglewood taught me lessons that went far beyond the classroom. I learned to cook, iron, and use yard equipment—not simply as chores, but as small acts of independence. Fueled by a desire to impress girls and earn a little pocket cash, I started cutting lawns around the neighborhood and even enrolled in a home economics class, teeming with girls—the kind of strategic move only a teenage boy with a plan could devise.

But life in Inglewood wasn't all innocence. Gang activity loomed large in the neighborhood, and though I never fully embraced that world, my older brother's reputation as "Player Ray" offered me a protective shield. His name carried weight, and as his younger brother, I learned the importance of street smarts—an education I would later fuse with formal academics to navigate diverse environments and connect with all types of people.

By 1982, I graduated junior high school. At my mother's insistence, I moved to live with my father in Los Angeles, a shift that would alter my perspective. In this new environment near Echo Park, I encountered a predominantly Latino community while being bused to a largely white school in the San Fernando Valley. It was a cultural collision that forced me to adapt quickly and understand differences—and similarities—between people.

That same year, I got my first job at Baskin-Robbins in Hollywood, scooping ice cream under the California sun. It was during this time I also joined the LAPD Hollywood Division's Explorer Scout program and met my first girlfriend, an older Caucasian girl from a different world. This relationship was my first real glimpse into the complexities of relationships, showing me firsthand how culture and background shape us and, sometimes, bring us together despite perceived divides.

Coming of Age (Ages 16-20)

The freedom of youth was marked by milestones that would shape the man I was becoming. Learning to drive opened up new worlds for me, and my first car—a 1969 tan VW Square back—became a symbol of independence and possibility. I graduated high school in 1985 and later earned an Associate of Arts degree from Santa Monica City College in 1989. But it wasn't a smooth journey. My position as a police cadet with the city of Santa Monica taught me my first real lessons in accountability. When I found myself on academic probation, I had to dig deep, doubling down on my efforts to meet the required GPA. Graduating with a 3.4 GPA felt like a victory—not just academically, but personally, proving to myself that I could rise to meet challenges head-on.

CHAPTER 4
BUILDING A LIFE

Build your own dreams,
or someone else will hire you to build theirs.

– Farraj Gray

Early Adulthood (Ages 20-25)

In the early '90s, I found myself at a crossroads, ready to chart a course with a clear vision for my future. Joining the US Coast Guard Reserves in 1990 was a pivotal decision, one that affirmed my commitment to public service and provided a sense of purpose and discipline that I had craved. The camaraderie, the structure, and the call to serve were not just duties I fulfilled, but experiences that profoundly shaped my character.

By 1993, I proudly graduated from California State University, Long Beach, with a degree in Criminal Justice and Security Management. This achievement was more than just a diploma; it was the culmination of years of hard work, late nights, and sacrifices. It was a key that opened doors to opportunities I had only dreamed of, and it symbolized a promise to myself to never settle for less than what I was capable of achieving.

During this time, I also began to explore my entrepreneurial instincts. I took satisfaction in small victories—designing and executing security plans, offering consultancy services, and finding innovative solutions that meet clients' needs. These early ventures were the seedlings of what would later become a full-fledged business, and they fueled a growing confidence in my ability to turn ideas into reality.

These years were also marked by personal growth and reflection. I learned to balance the demands of education, service, and budding professional interests with my personal life, discovering the importance of nurturing relationships along the way. It was a delicate dance, one that taught me the value of resilience, adaptability, and the power of perseverance.

These experiences collectively laid the groundwork for the entrepreneurial and leadership roles I would embrace in the years to come—roles that would challenge me, enrich me, and ultimately define the next chapters of my life.

Entrepreneurial Ventures and Family Life (Ages 25-30)

The thrill of purchasing my first home in North Hills, nestled in the San Fernando Valley, was a defining moment. It wasn't just bricks and mortar; it was a symbol of my hard work, a tangible representation of the financial stability I had strived for, and the beginning of my journey into asset building. The pride of ownership was immense, a feeling of accomplishment that fueled my entrepreneurial spirit even further.

I had always been brimming with ideas, a mind constantly churning with possibilities. Inspired by mentors and driven by an innate desire to create something of my own, I finally took the leap. Leaving the perceived security of my city job was a gamble, one that many around me questioned. "You'll never get ahead with a 3-5% raise," a former part-time employer, now a successful business owner, had told me. "It's best if you're the owner, the one signing the checks." His words resonated deeply, giving me the courage to bet on myself.

Armed with my college education and the practical experience gained from part-time security work, I poured my energy into launching Duncan Security Consultants Inc. (DSCI). It started as a spark, an idea ignited in the humble setting of my living room. From those modest beginnings, DSCI grew into something I could barely have imagined. We expanded to multiple states and even internationally, with several offices and a team of around 300 employees, generating an annual revenue of approximately $4.5 million. Building DSCI from the ground up wasn't just a business venture; it was a testament to my resilience, my vision, and my unwavering belief in the power of hard work.

Even amidst the whirlwind of building a business, the desire for a family of my own remained a constant undercurrent. I approached dating with intention, seeking a partner who shared my values and desire to settle down. This conscious decision reflected a growing awareness of the kind of life I wanted to create, one that balanced professional success with the joys of family life.

In 1997, amidst the demands of running a business and searching for a life partner, I embarked on a new academic challenge, enrolling in a Master of Public Administration program at California State University, Northridge. The thirst for knowledge and the drive to push myself intellectually remained a constant force, a testament to my belief in lifelong learning and personal growth. This period was a whirlwind of activity, a testament to my capacity to juggle multiple passions and commitments while striving to create a life rich with purpose and meaning. The closing of DSCI after ten years, due to lost contracts and my recall to active duty in the USCG following the 9/11 attacks, marked the end of an era, but also the beginning of a new chapter filled with unforeseen challenges and opportunities.

Personal and Professional Realignment (Ages 30-35)

As I crossed into my thirties, the complexity of balancing personal aspirations with professional commitments began to take shape in earnest. In 1997, I married Molly, marking the start of a deeply significant chapter in my life. A year later, we were blessed with our first child, a baby girl named Megan. This period was a whirlwind of new experiences and responsibilities that tested my ability to juggle the demands of a growing family with those of an expanding business.

The challenge of fatherhood was profound, especially without a male role model to guide me. I found myself navigating the delicate art of balance — striving to be present for my family while managing the rapid growth of Duncan Security Consultants Inc. The learning curve was steep, and the stakes were high. My main focus was to provide for my family in every way I could, yet I often felt torn between the office and home.

Molly and I decided that it would be best for our family if she stayed home with the children while I worked. This decision, though financially straining, allowed for stability at home but placed an immense pressure on me to succeed professionally. I did well in providing the material needs for my family, but I frequently lamented not being present enough, not being involved in the day-to-day moments that make up family life.

In the midst of these personal challenges, I achieved a significant milestone by graduating with a Master's degree from California State University, Northridge in 1999. This achievement was a first among the "Duncan kids," and it filled me with pride and a renewed sense of purpose. That same year, I earned my commission as a reserve Ensign in the US Coast Guard, marking the beginning of a deeply fulfilling aspect of my career.

The turn of the millennium brought more changes. In 2000, I was called to active duty with the US Coast Guard and reported to Headquarters in Washington, DC. There, I was assigned to the office of Maritime Prevention and Policy, which highlighted significant gaps in emergency response capabilities. My time at HQ was not only a period of professional growth but also of historical significance. I was part of the team that started the Maritime Security and Response Team, witnessing and contributing to its evolution from concept to operational reality, forging many lifelong friendships along the way.

Furthermore, I had the honor of serving on the Department of Homeland Security (DHS) integration team, a pivotal group tasked with merging several agencies under one umbrella to enhance national security. This role was yet another startup experience, albeit on a national scale, and it taught me invaluable lessons about leadership and innovation in high-stakes environments.

In 2002, our family grew again with the birth of our second daughter, Hailey, and soon after, we relocated to Washington, DC. This move came at a time when our third child, finally a boy, we named Kyle, joined our family. This period was a testament to the relentless pace of change and the constant need for adaptation. It was a time filled with seminal moments, both in my personal life and professional career, each demanding a recalibration of priorities and a deeper understanding of what it means to lead, to love, and to succeed.

Navigating Change and Heartbreak (Ages 35-40)

The years between 2007 and 2008 marked a turning point in my life, one that would forever alter the course of my personal and professional journey. After a tumultuous period of separation, I found myself facing the reality of divorce from Molly. It was a heart-wrenching decision, emotionally charged and filled with what-ifs that echoed in my mind. Leaving active service in the US Coast Guard and resigning my full-time officer commission was a bittersweet transition, as I shifted to a part-time reserve role. It felt like trading in one identity for another, navigating the complexities of both personal loss and professional reinvention.

I accepted a Vice President position at Pinkerton Government Services Inc. and relocated to Los Angeles. This new role was a beacon of opportunity in the midst of chaos, yet it came with the heavy burden of living bi-coastal. I was determined to remain actively involved in my children's lives, despite the physical distance that often separated us. The struggle was palpable; the emotional weight of the divorce and the challenges my kids faced in adapting to life without both parents together weighed heavily on my heart.

Court summons and petty disputes with my former wife became a routine that I had to navigate, a constant reminder of the difficulties we faced in co-parenting effectively. There was an undeniable tension, a lack of alignment between us that made everything more complicated. While I recognized that she was a good person and a loving mother, her decisions often felt misaligned with what was best for the children. We found ourselves wasting time and resources on disputes that could have been better channeled into supporting our kids and healing ourselves.

Amidst this turmoil, my oldest daughter came to live with me on the West Coast, offering a glimmer of hope and connection. Yet, even this positive change didn't shield us from the emotional upheaval that came with our family's restructuring. I often had to keep my lawyer on retainer, not out of malice, but as a necessary measure to protect my focus on what truly mattered—my children, my career, my health, and the budding new relationship that offered some semblance of stability.

Every year, I made attempts to set a level with my former wife. Each conversation seemed to fall flat, a testament to the difficulties we faced in finding common ground. I wanted to foster a cooperative spirit for the kids' sake, to create an environment where they could thrive amidst the challenges of our divorce. Despite our differences, I genuinely wished her well and hoped for her happiness. Over time, we learned to interact periodically for the sake of our children's activities, focusing on their needs while trying to navigate our complex relationship.

This chapter of my life was marked by heartache but also by resilience. It was a time of learning to redefine family, adapting to new realities, and finding strength in the face of adversity. Through it all, the love I had for my children remained a guiding light, illuminating the path ahead, even when the road felt uncertain and fraught with challenges.

CHAPTER 5
NAVIGATING NEW HORIZONS

Every new beginning comes from some other beginning's end.

– Seneca

Embracing New Beginnings and Challenges (Ages 40-45)

With an open heart and a newfound sense of clarity, I embraced the idea of commitment once more when I married Liz in 2011. This union felt like a second chance, an opportunity to build a family that included her son, Jordan, adding a new dynamic and warmth to our lives. It was a step forward, a leap into the unknown, but this time, I was ready. The lessons learned from my past had equipped me with the understanding that love requires both vulnerability and strength.

As I settled into this new chapter, my professional life continued to evolve. I remained dedicated to my roles at Pinkerton Government Services and in the US Coast Guard Reserves, but the demands of corporate travel began to escalate dramatically, increasing from 40% to 90%. This change, while challenging, reignited a long-dormant passion for the entertainment industry that I had first glimpsed in my youth.

Reflecting on my teenage years spent in acting classes, I felt a pull back to that creative energy. Liz, immersed in the entertainment business herself, became a source of inspiration and encouragement. The skills I had once dabbled in began to resurface, and the spark of creative ambition reignited within me. It was as if a window had opened, inviting me to explore a path I had never fully pursued, and the thought excited me.

However, life had its own plans, and in 2017, I was called back to active duty with the Coast Guard to respond to the devastating hurricanes—Harvey, Irma, and Maria—that wreaked havoc across several states and territories. Deploying to Texas, Missouri, Georgia, Puerto Rico, and the Virgin Islands, I found myself at the forefront of disaster response efforts. The weight of responsibility was immense; I led liaison efforts between various agencies, coordinating the response to ensure that help reached those in desperate need.

In these moments, I felt a deep sense of purpose and connection, a reminder of why I had chosen a life of service. It was a whirlwind of activity, but amidst the chaos, I found fulfillment in the work. Each deployment was a testament to resilience—the community's strength in adversity and the unwavering spirit of those affected.

These years were a profound blend of personal growth and professional dedication. I navigated the complexities of family life with Liz, Megan, Hailey, Kyle and Jordan while reawakening my passion for the arts and fulfilling my responsibilities in the Coast Guard. It was a time of embracing new beginnings while tackling the challenges that came with them, each experience adding depth and authenticity to my journey. Through it all, I realized that love, service, and creativity could coexist, enriching my life in ways I had yet to fully comprehend.

Pursuing Purpose and Connection (Ages 45-50)

In my mid-forties, I found myself in a constant state of exploration, ever on the lookout for professional opportunities that would align with my passions and values. It was during this period that a group of friends from my inner circle introduced me to Kappa Alpha Psi Fraternity Inc. in the fall of 2011. They saw something in me that I hadn't fully recognized yet—a potential to contribute to a legacy of brotherhood and service. Joining the fraternity became a transformative aspect of my life, offering not just fellowship but also a platform for leadership and community engagement.

The fraternity's mission resonated deeply with my own beliefs. It provided a space for collaboration, where teamwork became the backbone of meaningful community service activities. Through mentoring young men around the world, I discovered a profound sense of fulfillment. It was a chance to give back, to share the lessons I had learned along my journey, and to help shape the next generation of leaders. This commitment to mentorship became intertwined with the very core of who I am, igniting a passion within me to foster growth and inspire others.

Alongside my involvement with Kappa Alpha Psi, my professional life continued to flourish. I remained dedicated to my roles at Pinkerton and in the Coast Guard Reserves, but I also embraced a myriad of new opportunities that expanded my horizons. I ventured into acting, taking on roles that allowed me to express my creativity and connect with diverse narratives. As a technical advisor and producer, I applied my experiences to shape stories that resonated with audiences, marrying my past with my present in exciting ways.

Writing became another outlet for my thoughts and experiences, a cathartic process that allowed me to articulate the complexities of my life journey. I also stepped into the role of adjunct professor, sharing my knowledge with students eager to carve their paths in the world. This multifaceted career not only enriched my resume but also provided a sense of purpose that fueled my passions.

These years were a balancing act of professional growth and personal connection, each role I took on adding layers of depth to my identity. It was a time of exploration, where the pursuit of purpose intertwined with the importance of community and mentorship. I learned that success is not measured solely by titles or accolades but by the impact we have on others and the legacy we leave behind. Through it all, I embraced the journey, recognizing that every opportunity was a chance to learn, grow, and contribute to a greater good.

Navigating Heartbreak and New Horizons (Ages 50-55)

Reflecting on the promises Liz and I made to each other, it breaks my heart to acknowledge that we did not fulfill our vow to never divorce. The dissolution of our marriage in 2018 left me personally devastated, and it came at a tumultuous time in my life. I had recently been confronted with the stark realization that I was showing some indicators of PTSD from my last deployment. A close colleague's observation about my mental health struck a nerve, prompting a promise to myself to seek help upon my return stateside.

In the aftermath of our separation, I sought professional guidance, and the confirmation of significant stressors was a wake-up call I could no longer ignore. The therapist encouraged me to begin therapeutic work as soon as possible, a suggestion that became a vital lifeline. The end of my marriage acted as a trigger, unearthing unresolved trauma that I had learned to shelve for years. I found myself on a roller coaster of emotions, grappling with both the end of a significant relationship and the buried pain that resurfaced.

Taking time to simplify my life became essential. A wise friend and fellow comrade, who had urged me to promise I would seek help upon my return, provided me with the support I desperately needed. I felt immense gratitude for his intervention; it shifted my focus inward, prompting me to confront the emotional baggage I had long neglected. Armed with new tools to manage life's challenges, I began to tackle my past and address the stressors that had once overwhelmed me.

In 2020, with newfound clarity and a commitment to self-care, I cautiously stepped back into the dating world. It was a transformative experience, meeting lovely women over the following years. I found myself entering into an exclusive relationship that seemed to be progressing positively. However, I knew that navigating this new landscape required a thoughtful approach. I developed a process to help me safely and enjoyably explore the possibilities of dating while remaining grounded in my journey of healing.

Amidst these personal developments, I received an incredible professional opportunity in 2020—a quick-moving assignment to Haiti that promised new challenges and adventures. After thorough consultations with my work, family, and girlfriend, I decided to embrace this three-year assignment. It felt like a leap of faith, a chance to immerse myself in a new culture while furthering my career, all while dedicating myself to personal growth.

As I moved forward, I learned that life is a series of transitions, each accompanied by its own set of challenges and rewards. The lessons from heartbreak and healing became guiding principles in this next chapter, and I embraced the journey ahead, knowing that the possibilities before me were vast and filled with potential.

Closing a Chapter, Embracing a New Journey (Ages 56 to Present)

After years of careful deliberation, I made the bittersweet decision to retire from the U.S. Coast Guard Reserve, bringing a 34-year career of service to a close. It wasn't a decision I took lightly. The past few years and my final assignments gave me the clarity I needed: it was time. People often ask how you know when it's time to let go of something so integral to your life, and my answer is simple—you just know. Filing the paperwork was both exciting and surreal, a mixture of pride and anticipation for the next chapter.

The timing aligned well with the Coast Guard's personnel system, which made space for my departure, allowing me the grace to pass the torch and move forward without lingering obligations. It was a clean break, a moment of closure, and a chance to embrace a life that wasn't tethered to uniform schedules, deployments, or service commitments. For the first time in decades, I could shift my focus inward—toward family, personal health, and the pursuit of a well-rounded, meaningful life.

The official ceremony in Portsmouth, Virginia, marked the culmination of this journey. It was a poignant moment, surrounded by family and friends who had supported me along the way. My daughter Megan summed it up perfectly when she said, "Dad, you ended the longest relationship you've ever had." Her words hit me harder than I expected, and as they sank in, I felt the weight of both pride and loss. I looked at her, smiled, and gave her a big hug. She was right—the Coast Guard had been my steadfast companion for over three decades. A part of me wished that my first marriage could have claimed that title instead, or at least come close, but life has its own way of unfolding.

As I step into this new phase of life, I've embraced the beauty of slowing down, of being intentional. I'm taking my time to build a promising relationship with someone special, holding close to my mom's wise words about truly experiencing "all the seasons" together—maybe even two rounds of them. There's no rush, just a commitment to enjoying the process of getting to know each other fully and authentically.

Geographically, I've found joy in what I call my "trifecta of living," splitting my time between Los Angeles, Virginia, and the Dominican Republic. Each place offers something unique—one has family and fraternity engagements, another has professional opportunities, while others provide rest, recreation, and cherished community connections. It's a lifestyle that reflects the essence of who I am, blending purpose, adventure, and relaxation.

Professionally, I've embraced a part-time schedule that aligns with my passions and interests. Working as a producer, creator, advisor, and consultant in the entertainment and security-emergency management sectors allows me to stay engaged without overcommitting. I only take on projects that excite me and bring joy, ensuring that this stage of life remains as fulfilling as it is balanced.

This next chapter is not about rushing to fill a void or chasing something fleeting. It's about savoring the freedom to choose, to connect, and to live authentically. I've come to realize that endings are not failures—they're transitions, opportunities to reflect on what was and embrace what could be. For the first time in a long while, I feel unburdened, hopeful, and ready to write the next page of my story with intention, joy, and purpose.

Chapter 6
MY PROFESSIONAL EXPERIENCE

The best way to find yourself is to lose yourself in the service of others.

– Mahatma Gandhi

My professional journey has been anything but conventional—a voyage guided by a commitment to service, a thirst for growth, and a passion for contributing to something larger than myself. From the sun-drenched shores of California to the bustling ports of Haiti, my career has been a diverse tapestry woven with experiences ranging from the rigorous structure of military command to the dynamic challenges of the private sector.

This journey began in 1990 when I joined the U.S. Coast Guard. Boot camp at Cape May, New Jersey, was my initiation into a world of discipline, purpose, and unshakeable camaraderie. This marked the start of a 34-year adventure that would take me from enlisted seaman to a Senior Reserve Officer and Branch Chief at LANTAREA CG-35, where I oversaw future operations for the eastern half of the United States, the Caribbean, and critical missions across Europe, Africa, and Southwest Asia.

Earning the title of "mustang," a rare achievement signifying my transition from enlisted ranks to a senior commissioned officer, stands as one of my proudest milestones. The years spent in the Coast Guard instilled in me a deep understanding of leadership—one that extends far beyond the simple act of command. It's about empathy, adaptability, and the ability to inspire those around you, even amid uncertainty. I learned that true leadership is not about wielding power, but about empowering others.

My roles were as varied as the seas themselves. As the Senior Defense Official and Defense Attaché in Haiti, I served as the principal advisor to the U.S. Ambassador and the Department of Defense's representative, navigating complex international relations with diplomacy and tact. In Honolulu, I oversaw the readiness of reserve forces across the Hawaiian Islands, ensuring our preparedness for missions ranging from search and rescue to national security. As an Emergency Preparedness Liaison Officer for FEMA Region 9, I collaborated with local, state, and federal agencies to coordinate disaster response plans, ensuring continuity during crises.

The aftermath of the 9/11 attacks stands out as a pivotal moment. Called to active duty, I contributed to drafting the Maritime Transportation Security Act (MTSA), shaping policies that would protect critical infrastructure and enhance national security for years to come. The weight of responsibility was immense, but the knowledge that our work would have a lasting impact on our nation's safety was profoundly humbling. Whether leading maritime investigations, managing contingency plans, or co-chairing groundbreaking initiatives like integrating divers and sonar technology to enhance port security, my Coast Guard career was defined by a commitment to innovation, resilience, and unwavering service. I have had the opportunity to work with every three and four alphabet agencies during my professional experience.

Transitioning to Civilian Leadership: Navigating New Shores

Transitioning from the military to the civilian world presented its own set of challenges, but it also offered a chance to apply my skills and experiences in new arenas. I sought roles that allowed me to combine strategic leadership with a commitment to safety and security. My journey became a metaphor for a ship navigating different seas: the same vessel, the same captain, but with changing charts and winds.

As Director of Safety, Security, and Environmental Compliance for Nautilus International, I oversaw compliance across marine terminals in the United States. This involved risk management, safety protocol development, and fostering a culture of continuous improvement. Collaborating with stakeholders ranging from federal and state agencies to senior corporate leaders, I learned to navigate the complexities of the private sector while maintaining the same dedication to mission-focused leadership that had defined my military career. My work with Nautilus also extended to influencing national policy as a voting member of the Area Maritime Security Committee for the ports of Los Angeles and Long Beach, contributing to the safety and security of some of the busiest ports globally.

In my role as Vice President and Global Account Manager for Pinkerton Government Services, I managed a multimillion-dollar contract with Boeing, overseeing security operations across 35 sites in 15 states. Leading a team of over 800 members, I focused on implementing best practices, conducting audits, and resolving complex operational challenges while ensuring strict compliance with laws and regulations. This required a different type of navigation, but the core values remained the same: commitment, service, and excellence.

Giving Back: A Commitment to Mentorship and Community

My commitment has extended beyond professional achievements. Serving on the Board of Directors for the Valley Economic Development Corp (VEDC), a $30 million non-profit, allowed me to contribute to supporting small businesses through financial services and community outreach. Advising on financial audits, fundraising, and organizational policies gave me immense fulfillment in empowering others to succeed. Teaching counterterrorism and intelligence courses as an Adjunct Professor has been equally rewarding, sharing my knowledge and experiences with military, law enforcement, and emergency management personnel. This is my way of paying forward the mentorship I received and nurturing the next generation of leaders.

Reflections on an Unconventional Path: Looking Ahead

Looking back, my career path may seem unconventional, but it is deeply rooted in intention and purpose. From the decks of Coast Guard vessels and landslide units to the intricate dynamics of corporate boardrooms, I have embraced challenges that have pushed me to grow and allowed me to make a meaningful impact. For a complete listing of my professional achievements and positions, please refer to the Appendix. My journey has been defined by connection—connecting with people, bridging industries, and finding common ground between seemingly disparate roles. Whether leading a security initiative, drafting national policy, or mentoring aspiring leaders, I have stayed true to the values of collaboration, adaptability, and integrity.

As I approach the next chapter, I am filled with gratitude for the experiences that have shaped me and the people who have inspired me along the way. My professional journey has been more than a career; it has been a calling, and one that I have answered with every ounce of dedication and passion I possess.

CHAPTER 7
"THE MIDDLE"; LIFE STARTED, AND "MY LONGEST RELATIONSHIP"

True heroism is remarkably sober, very undramatic. It is not the urge to surpass all others at whatever cost, but the urge to serve others at whatever cost.

– Arthur Ashe

Setting Sail

Life took a dramatic turn when I embarked on my full-time journey with the U.S. Coast Guard. This wasn't a decision made lightly; it emerged from family discussions and a shared desire for unity and growth. My wife and I made the bold choice to move across the country, trading the familiar sunlit streets of Los Angeles for the historical heart of Washington, D.C. Leaving behind friends, family, and the company I had painstakingly built was a sacrifice, but one made in the name of our shared future.

Letting go of my business was particularly difficult. It was more than just a company; it was a piece of me, a testament to years of hard work and nurtured relationships. However, the inherent conflict of interest demanded this sacrifice. With my mother stepping in to manage, the company eventually closed its doors, marking the end of an era for both of us. Rather than dwelling on the loss, I chose to focus on the invaluable lessons learned and the pride of having created opportunities for others. This experience underscored the delicate balance between personal ambition and professional duty.

Charting a Course

My Coast Guard career began with the rigorous training of boot camp in Cape May and Port Security School in Yorktown. Starting as a boat crewman, I steadily progressed to become a law enforcement boarding officer at Station Channel Island Harbor, experiences that prepared me for the challenges to come. In 1999, encouraged by mentors who saw my potential, I transitioned into a commissioned officer, taking on new responsibilities with the Naval Coastal Warfare and Harbor Defense Unit 114.

A defining chapter of my life unfolded at the U.S. Naval Dive & Salvage Center, a crucible of mental and physical endurance. At the time, I had no idea I was about to become the first African American officer to complete this demanding program. That realization came later, when a colleague, after looking into the history, told me I had broken barriers in ways I hadn't even considered. True to form, I initially brushed it off. Celebrating my accomplishments had never been my style. Whether it was surviving dive school or earning promotions through the ranks, I tended to view them as steps in the larger mission, not as moments to pause and reflect.

Dive school demanded more than physical strength; it tested the limits of resilience and resolve. Each evolution, whether mastering Boyle's Law and empirical charts in the classroom or surviving "pool week," where any sign of fear turned you into prey, pushed me to my limits. One of the most profound lessons I learned was how to become comfortable with the idea of drowning—not in a literal sense, but in surrendering to discomfort and fear. The training forced me to trust the process, even as I struggled against my instincts to surface. That trust was critical, not just for success in dive school but as a mindset for overcoming challenges in life.

The deep dive qualification remains etched in my memory as the ultimate test. Sick and congested, I fought through every instinct to stop, forcing my body to adapt as I descended ~150 feet. When I surfaced, blood trickled from my ear—a brutal reminder of how much I had endured. My instructor, a seasoned Navy diver, simply said, "That was 'Hooyah.' It wasn't just the physical feat he recognized but the mental fortitude to persevere when every fiber of my being screamed to quit.

What set this experience apart wasn't just the rigor—it was the psychological toll. Dive school tested my ability to stay calm under relentless pressure, whether completing complex underwater tasks or navigating unexpected challenges. I learned to embrace discomfort and uncertainty, to focus on small victories, and to keep moving forward.

Years later, the significance of that achievement began to sink in—not through my own reflection, but through the pride of my kids. One of my daughters, during a Black History Month celebration at school, shared the story with her classmates. Her words brought my journey full circle, showing me the impact it had beyond my own life. In her eyes, I saw what this milestone truly represented: a legacy of perseverance, resilience, and hope for those who come next. Like a lighthouse beam cutting through the fog, my achievement illuminated a path for others to follow.

Navigating New Waters

Transitioning to the reserves in 2008 presented another turning point. Balancing civilian aspirations with my commitment to service was a constant juggling act, but it allowed me to explore diverse roles while maintaining my connection to the Coast Guard. As the Senior Reserve Officer of Response at Sector Los Angeles-Long Beach, managing a team of over 90 reservists, I honed my leadership skills and learned the critical importance of adaptability.

Assignments in Hawaii further enriched my understanding of cultural richness and the power of community. The "Ohana" spirit resonated deeply, reinforcing my belief in the importance of family and shared experiences. These lessons proved invaluable, shaping my approach to leadership and service.

In 2020, my career took an unexpected and exciting turn when I was nominated to serve as a U.S. Diplomat and Defense Attaché in Haiti. This role was both an honor and a weighty responsibility, bridging my military experience with the world of international diplomacy. Serving as a Senior DoD Advisor to the Ambassador and collaborating with defense and intelligence leaders from around the globe demanded resilience and a nuanced understanding of diplomacy. Each challenge faced in Haiti was met with the knowledge that I was contributing to something larger than myself.

Coming Ashore

Looking back, my Coast Guard journey has been a tapestry woven with threads of service, sacrifice, and success. I'm deeply grateful for my family's unwavering support throughout, providing an anchor amidst the often-turbulent waters of my responsibilities. Armed with degrees in Criminal Justice-Security Management and Public Administration, I now stand ready to embrace the next chapter. Retirement isn't an end, but a new beginning—an opportunity to share my experiences, consult on new projects, and explore the world with fresh eyes. It's a chance to reflect on the voyages past and chart a course for the adventures that lie ahead.

CHAPTER 8
FAMILY AND COMMITMENT

*Other things may change us,
but we start and end with the family.*

– Anthony Brandt

Childhood Reflections

My childhood wasn't defined by material riches, but by the steadfast love and relentless dedication of a single mother raising five children. We always had a roof over our heads, clothes, food on the table, and our health needs met—a testament to my mother's unyielding work ethic and resourcefulness. My father was present at times, but his role was more rooted in providing financial support when with him, than emotional connection. Looking back, I've come to understand his limitations as a product of his own difficult upbringing. He carried the scars of his environment, and though it left an indelible mark on our family dynamics, I've learned to offer him grace. Over the years, he's made significant strides to improve as a father and a man. Opinionated and self-centered though he may remain, his willingness to grow has been meaningful.

Growing up as the middle child—and my mother's favorite, a fact made apparent by our striking physical resemblance—was a unique experience. My mother may have been the backbone of our family, but my older siblings presented distinct challenges. Without a steady father figure, they struggled to find their footing and often made unproductive choices. Despite our challenges, we lived in some of Inglewood's better neighborhoods—a true reflection of my mother's hard work. My father's contributions were primarily financial, especially during the times we spent with him. When my parents separated, my father left, and we stayed in the family home.

He was the "fun dad," but in retrospect, also a selfish one. The emotional toll he inflicted on my mother was significant trauma that was emotional rather than physical. Thankfully, my grandmother "Gi Gi" stepped in as a stabilizing influence. Her unwavering support for my mother and us provided the family with much-needed strength during difficult times.

At fifteen, I moved in with my father in Echo Park, a predominantly Mexican neighborhood in Los Angeles. This change was eye-opening, especially after having been bused to the San Fernando Valley, a mostly white area. Living in Echo Park introduced me to a vibrant culture and a community vastly different from what I had known. It was a pivotal moment that broadened my understanding of the world around me.

Family Dynamics and Struggles

As my siblings and I grew older, our relationships began to unravel. We drifted apart, both geographically and emotionally. My younger brother and sister stayed with my mother, while my younger sister spent some time with my father after he moved closer to South Los Angeles. My older brother, a formidable presence in Inglewood, faced his struggles, including a brief stint in juvenile detention. Despite this, I'm immensely proud of the man he's become, turning his life around completely. My older sister, Lannette, had her own battles—lifelong mental health challenges that led to estrangement from the family.

Then came Lannette's sudden death from a heart attack. Her passing was a heartbreaking loss, one that underscored the dysfunction that had long plagued our family. We were never truly a cohesive unit, something I came to understand more acutely by observing the close-knit families of my friends. Her death was a painful reminder of what we lacked but also a call to action for me to change the narrative.

Breaking the Cycle

Lannette's death ignited a fierce determination within me to break the cycle of disconnection and dysfunction. I refuse to let the same distance fester in my relationships with my own children and grandchildren. My commitment is to be deeply involved in their lives, fostering bonds that endure through triumphs and losses alike. I want us to be a family that leans on one another, celebrates together, and supports one another in hardship.

This resolve was evident during a recent family reunion in Chicago. Though tinged with sadness, it marked a hopeful new beginning. We're planning a Christmas visit with my father as well, taking intentional steps to rebuild and nurture our relationships. It's not easy to mend the fractures of the past, but I am committed to doing my part.

A New Legacy

My three children—Megan, Hailey, and Kyle—are now adults, and I couldn't be prouder of the people they've become. Megan, a creative force, is thriving as a Pilates instructor, photographer, entertainer, and entrepreneur. Hailey, a recent college graduate with a double major and a retired D1 volleyball player, has already started making her mark as a pre-delivery nurse. She's also expecting her first child later this year, making me a grandfather for the first time. Kyle, having just completed his BFA in Film and Fine Arts, is preparing to embark on an exciting career in the entertainment industry.

Each of them is healthy, productive, and kind-hearted. Even though I sometimes jokingly refer to them as my "YAKs" (young adult kids)—a nickname they've rejected—they've grown into respectful individuals, creative problem-solvers, and global thinkers. As they navigate adulthood, I cherish the new chapter in our relationship. There's something about being Duncan—a blend of charisma, a strong work ethic, and a touch of "fun factor"—that binds us, even as we've faced our challenges.

The Impact on My Children: Lessons in Presence and Redemption

Reflecting on the most personal aspects of my life, nothing weighs on me more than the impact my choices and circumstances had on my children. During my first marriage, the unraveling of the relationship was a painful process, and the hardest part was watching my kids struggle to understand why mom and dad were no longer together. I wanted so badly to shield them from that pain, to create a sense of normalcy, but I didn't always know how. I sacrificed parts of myself to ease their burden, but I realize now that what they needed most was for me to be fully present—a lesson I learned too late in those early years.

My son Kyle, in particular, carried the weight of those moments quietly. As a young boy, he didn't have the words to express what he was feeling, but he watched and listened to everything. I didn't always see it then, but he was processing it all in his own way. When I look back now, I hear his voice—soft but clear—sharing how he felt I wasn't always there. Those words cut deeply, even today. My daughter, too, has shared similar feelings. I see now how my focus on solving problems and moving forward—habits that served me well professionally—created distance in my personal life, especially with my children.

Those realizations have driven me to do better. Over the past 12 years, I've made a daily practice of reflection, grounding myself in gratitude and intentionally focusing on how I can show up for the people who matter most. My children are at the center of that effort. I've learned to celebrate their milestones in ways I never allowed myself to celebrate my own. I've encouraged them to experience life fully—to embrace opportunities I didn't have, like the freedom to immerse themselves in college life, to explore, and to grow without the constant pressure of responsibility.

My kids have been my greatest teachers, showing me the importance of presence and connection. Their resilience and love inspire me to keep growing, to make up for the moments I missed, and to create new ones together. I carry their voices with me every day, reminding me of what truly matters: being there, not just in the big moments, but in the small ones, too. They've taught me that redemption isn't about erasing the past—it's about building a better future, one moment at a time.

Moving Forward

This chapter reflects not only on family dynamics but on the resilience of the human spirit and the enduring power of love and connection. The challenges of my upbringing have fueled my determination to build a better future for my children and break the cycle of dysfunction that has overshadowed my family for generations. It's a journey that requires dedication, empathy, and a commitment to nurturing relationships with the people who matter most.

As I look to the future, I hold onto the belief that it's never too late to rewrite the story. Family is a constant work in progress, but it is always worth the effort. With each step, I strive to create a legacy of closeness, compassion, and love— a legacy I hope my children and grandchildren will carry forward.

Chapter 9
MARRIAGE; ANOTHER LEVEL OF COMMITMENT

Every relationship teaches you something important about yourself—whether it lasts a day, a year, or a lifetime.

— Unknown

Reflections on Marriage

Marriage has brought me not just honor and blessings but also formidable challenges. Having been married and divorced twice, I understand deeply that love is not just about feelings but about deliberate actions. Each of my former wives brought distinct qualities and cultural backgrounds that enriched my life—my first wife's Scandinavian heritage and my second wife's German roots both introduced me to new perspectives. Despite their intelligence, attractiveness, and inherent goodness, I've learned that a successful marriage hinges on both partners' active participation and unwavering commitment.

In reflecting on my marriages, I've come to understand that relationships are intricate mazes without a one-size-fits-all map. Numerous relationship books have offered valuable insights, yet the cornerstone of a lasting marriage, I've found, is the commitment to navigate these mazes together, facing challenges head-on. While the vows of "for better or for worse, in sickness and in health" are easy to say, truly living them out is where the real work lies.

Lessons Learned

In both marriages, we encountered numerous challenges that, regrettably, led to divorce. I acknowledge my role in these failures; I was not always the partner I strived to be. For instance, cultural differences in my first marriage often clouded our communication. There were times when instead of celebrating our differences, I let them become walls that added strain to our relationship.

Similarly, in my second marriage, the struggle to balance individual needs and unhealthy choices with our shared life was a constant battle. I recall prioritizing work over our relationship, mistakenly believing I was fulfilling my duties, yet I overlooked the critical emotional connection. This neglect taught me that sustaining a partnership requires more than love; it demands consistent effort, open communication, and a readiness to adapt.

Moving Forward

Looking back, I see relationships as dances where both partners must move in sync. It's not enough for one to lead while the other follows reluctantly; both must be willing to engage in the rhythm of life together. Throughout my journey, some have suggested that perhaps we ended our marriages too hastily, that perhaps we weren't prepared to move forward together. The marriages ended, the first with the first filing, the second with us both filing, that said, I preferred they didn't end and we found a way to grow and heal inside of the marriages. Now, I understand the importance of timing and readiness in a relationship—the right relationship is where both partners are enthusiastically running toward and servicing each other.

As I explore the realm of intentional dating once again, I find myself better equipped than ever. Always a relationship-oriented person, I now approach potential partners with a clearer understanding of what I want and need. Envisioning a metaphorical "dating show" in my mind, I carefully weigh each aspect of potential relationships, armed with insights from past experiences.

Currently, I strive to balance my time to make room for love, aiming for peace, positive energy, and happiness. I seek a healthy relationship where both individuals are committed to enriching each other's lives while adeptly managing life's realities.

A New Chapter

In this new chapter of my life, I cherish the lessons from my past marriages. I am committed to being a better partner—a person who communicates openly, celebrates cultural differences, and approaches relationships with intentionality. With each experience, much like a vine that strengthens over time, I hope to grow richer in understanding and more adept at nurturing meaningful connections.

As I look forward, I embrace the belief that love is a continuous action, active commitment to one another, and that words matter. Ready to engage in the beautiful dance of partnership once again, I run toward the future, hopeful to build a relationship grounded in mutual respect, admiration, healthy choices, spirituality and a shared commitment to growth.

Chapter 10
HIGHER LEARNING:
THE GIFT THAT KEEPS GIVING...

The beautiful thing about learning is that no one can take it away from you.

– B.B. King

Early Lessons

Education, I've come to understand, isn't confined to classrooms. It unfolds on the streets, in everyday situations, and through the people we meet. My life has been a continuous journey of learning, driven by innate curiosity and a hunger to know more, to be more. As a young man, however, school wasn't where I thrived. I vividly recall my father's bewildered expression when he discovered the discrepancies in my high school attendance records. My sheepish admission of boredom—a frequent escape into daydreams and gazing out the window—led to a stern reprimand. This wasn't merely about avoiding punishment; it was a moment of self-reflection that would profoundly change my approach to learning.

My father's disappointment, while initially painful, served as a pivotal wake-up call. The shame I felt at my lack of engagement spurred a profound shift in my attitude. It wasn't just about avoiding punishment; it was about recognizing the inherent value of education, something I had previously taken for granted. This newfound appreciation became crucial as I embarked on my journey to higher education.

Higher Education

I attended Santa Monica Community College and then California State University, Long Beach, where I earned my BS, followed by a Master's in Public Administration at California State University, Northridge. Becoming the first in my family to graduate from college brought immense pride, mingled with humbling reflections on the journey. Each step added to my understanding of the world and myself. The educational experiences provided me with a strong foundation and equipped me with valuable skills.

Lessons from the Streets

Yet, the streets also provided invaluable lessons that no formal education could. I learned to read the unspoken messages in people's gestures and expressions—skills honed further by academic courses in nonverbal communication. Sometimes, it felt like walking through a dense forest where the path wasn't always clear, but the ability to read subtle signs—a shift in tone, a glance, a gesture—kept me on track and out of harm's way. This knowledge became my shield and guide, helping me navigate tricky situations and avoid, or be ready for, potentially dangerous encounters.

Lifelong Learning

My curiosity never waned. It led me to consider a doctorate, and though I haven't yet decided on that path, the thrill of learning keeps it on the horizon. I've embraced every opportunity to expand my education through professional training academies, fellowships, and specialized courses. Each experience has been a stepping stone, not just in knowledge but in personal growth. I've learned that education isn't just about absorbing information; it's about applying it, challenging oneself, and learning from both successes and failures. It's about understanding that every person we meet has something to teach us, if we're willing to listen. The process of learning is continuous and deeply rewarding.

Reflection

Reflecting on my journey, I see how each phase of my education—from the disciplined settings of academia to the unpredictable lessons of the streets—has shaped me. Learning isn't just about personal achievement; it's about how we use that knowledge to engage with the world. As I continue to navigate life's complexities, my approach remains the same: stay curious, be open, and never stop learning. In this vast classroom of life, I am both a student and a teacher, eager to share the lessons I've learned and equally eager to discover new ones. The gift of learning is truly one that keeps on giving. It is a continuous process of growth and self-discovery.

CHAPTER 11
THE CREATIVITY SPACE; FREEDOM TO JUST BE...

The creative adult is the child who survived.
— Ursula K. Le Gui

From my earliest memories, creativity has been the lens through which I view the world. As the middle child, often caught between the boisterous personalities of my siblings, I found unique ways to forge my path, build consensus, and think outside the conventional box. My formative years were filled not just with action but with observation, absorbing the world in a way that was distinctly my own.

Interestingly, my parents once shared a story about my early years that perhaps best illustrates my innate drive for efficiency and clarity. They told me that as a baby, I bypassed the usual babbling phase and, instead, around the age of two or three, I simply started speaking clear words. While I don't have personal recollections of this, it's a tale confirmed by various family members. It seems I was absorbing language all along, only choosing to express myself when I could communicate effectively—why waste time with baby talk when you can articulate exactly what you need?

This early anecdote hints at a lifelong preference for efficiency and clarity—a drive that continues to shape my creative process. My love for languages, cultures, and communities isn't a mere interest but a core part of who I am. Authenticity and originality ignite my passion; repetition and the status quo stifle it. This focus on impactful results over minor details is reflected in my "80-20" (and sometimes "90-10") approach to life. I prioritize significant impacts over minor details, especially when a project requires intense focus or involves inherent risks. This approach, a natural extension of my early preference for direct communication, has shaped both my personal and professional life, pushing me toward innovation and unexpected creative solutions.

My outputs—whether in art, leisure, or professional endeavors—frequently look different from those of my family and friends. I envision my life as a river that creatively meanders through obstacles toward a path of fulfillment, sometimes encountering more barriers than expected. Life indeed throws curveballs, as evidenced by my experience with flight school applications. When I wasn't accepted into the Coast Guard's flight program, I initially felt a wave of disappointment wash over me. However, I didn't let that setback halt my momentum. Instead, I pivoted to dive school, embracing the new challenge with open arms and completing the program with fervor. This experience reinforced my belief that every challenge can lead me to new and unexpected opportunities.

The realm of creativity in which I live, work, and play is vibrant and dynamic. It becomes even more exhilarating when I have the opportunity to collaborate with others. There's something profoundly rewarding about developing an idea from a mere spark into a full-fledged concept that evokes emotion in others. The process of creation, from inception to realization, is a dance of collaboration, each step building on the last, culminating in a shared celebration of what we've collectively brought to life.

Looking ahead, I see my life's next chapter as a continuation of this collaborative spirit, infused with good energy and dedicated to telling stories that matter. Living, in itself, influences great stories, breeds conflict, and forges characters strong enough to inspire. I look forward to each new day as a fresh page, ready to be filled with vivid narratives crafted not just by me but by the many voices I encounter.

Each experience, each interaction, is an opportunity to learn and grow. Thus, as I advance in this journey, my commitment remains steadfast: to live creatively, embracing each challenge as an opportunity, and to continue flowing like a river—sometimes calm, sometimes turbulent, but always moving forward.

In this creativity space, I am reminded that the freedom to just be is not merely about self-expression; it's about connecting with others and the world around me. It's about embracing the unpredictable journey of life and allowing my creativity to flourish in every moment.

CHAPTER 12
COMMUNITY AND SPIRITUALITY; A PLACE TO CONNECT

The greatness of a community is most accurately measured by the compassionate actions of its members.

– Coretta Scott King

My life has been a tapestry woven from the threads of community, each unique and profoundly influential. From my family's familiar embrace, to the camaraderie I found in the youth police explorer program at age thirteen, I have always been drawn to diverse groups that offer invaluable lessons and shape my perspectives.

The Impact of Community

Joining the youth police explorer program was a revelation. It introduced me to a world different from my own—a boy scout-like experience integrated with the local police department. With my father's permission, I eagerly stepped into this new community, eager to learn not just about policing concepts but about teamwork, service, and the power of vulnerability in a safe environment.

That program became a crucible for personal growth. It instilled in me a deep appreciation for service, not only to my community but to myself. Amidst drills and training, I learned the importance of organization, discipline, and responsibility—lessons that extend far beyond those early experiences. I made lasting friendships, discovered my first part-time job, and found my first girlfriend. The ripple effects of that experience continue to shape my life.

Evolving Spirituality

My spiritual journey began in the Catholic Church, a faith I embraced before my wedding in 1997. Initially, the connection felt profound; God seemed ever-present. However, as the horrific stories of priestly abuse came to light, I found myself questioning the institution. My faith evolved, moving away from dogma toward a more personal, non-denominational practice grounded in Christian values.

I believe in something larger than myself, a spiritual force that transcends human understanding. Throughout my life, unexpected intersections with people have led to life-altering opportunities, moments when I felt divinely guided, and other times when I felt utterly alone. These experiences have taught me that when things don't go as planned, there's always a lesson to be learned.

Lessons of Resilience

One significant moment stands out: a night training exercise in San Diego. During a physically demanding descent from a Coast Guard helicopter, I faced a dangerous swing that threatened to send me into the water. In that split second, I found an unexpected surge of strength, allowing me to land safely. My training helped, but the timing felt like divine intervention—a "God wink."

These experiences remind me that the threads of community, faith, and unexpected moments continuously weave through my life, shaping my perspectives. They reinforce the importance of resilience and the enduring presence of something greater than ourselves.

CHAPTER 13
FORGED IN FIRE:
FINDING STRENGTH IN ADVERSITY

The world breaks everyone, and afterward, many are strong at the broken places.

– Ernest Hemingway

At a young age, I was struck by a seismic shock: a false criminal accusation. This challenge could have shattered my spirit, but instead, it was supported by a foundation of a skilled lawyer, my mother's unwavering love, and the loyalty of my friends. This harrowing experience, while painfully transformative, forged an unyielding fortitude within me. It opened my eyes to the pervasive nature of prejudice and ignited a fierce determination to triumph over adversity.

The burden of injustice weighed on my shoulders like a heavy cloak, suffocating and oppressive. Facing the accusation, uncertainty and fear of judgment based on falsehoods left an indelible mark on me. Feelings of anger, hurt, and betrayal were intense and palpable. Although tempted to seek vengeance through legal means, I realized this would not bring peace. Instead, I chose a path of quiet defiance, allowing my actions and integrity to speak volumes. This ordeal, rather than breaking me, became a beacon, illuminating the dark corners of bias and injustice that I was determined to eradicate.

Navigating life's complexities—the good, the bad, and everything in between—is truly an art form. I learned through school, personal interactions, my parents' struggles, observing others, and intense training environments, influenced by the wise counsel of my mentors. I embraced the principle that quitting was never an option; instead, one should tirelessly "work the problem." I committed to learning from my mistakes, understanding that repetitive errors steal both time and progress. I adopted the mindset of "failing forward," viewing setbacks not as endings, but as opportunities for learning and growth.

Each challenge taught me more about my own resilience. Growing up in a fragmented family, contending with societal labels, and navigating challenging environments where success seemed elusive—these experiences reinforced that true strength does not come from avoiding hardships but from confronting them directly. Whether tackling self-doubt or professional obstacles, my perseverance turned potential failures into lessons. Resilience, I learned, is not an unyielding boulder but a flowing river, carving its path through the landscape of challenges with grace and determination. This approach has been the cornerstone of my achievements and continues to guide me through life's unpredictable journey.

Life's challenges are incessant, and I have learned to meet them head-on. Embracing discomfort and speaking truth to power often resulted in unexpected acceptance of my honesty. I found solace in intentional stillness, in those quiet moments of reflection that provided much-needed clarity and perspective. I actively disrupted stagnant situations, replacing negative energies with a positive intent. I discovered that good energy acts as medicine, healing and invigorating. Daily acts of kindness, such as bringing joy to someone else's day, proved to be potent antidotes to negativity.

My journey is also shaped by the powerful examples of resilience from those around me. My mother, overcoming a challenging childhood, emerged with a spirit of indomitable tenacity, teaching me the invaluable lessons of hard work and sacrifice. My father, initially embodying the carefree "fun dad," evolved over time into a figure of empathy and thoughtfulness. My dad was is a great example of working hard to retire and he shared some sound advice to take care of your credit and teeth.

Despite their imperfections, my parents did their best with the knowledge they had. My own path, woven through various educational and professional experiences, false accusations, and the raw realities of life's harsher sides, has been rich with learning. Encountering societal judgment based on my appearance and witnessing the struggles of loved ones within the legal system has crafted a resilience in me that is both quiet and powerful.

Intentional stillness, daily reflection, gratitude, and thankfulness are the ingredients to a life filled with good energy, peace, and happiness. The answers to life's questions are always there; often, we just need to step back, listen, and be willing to grow and change. This is my alchemical formula for a well-lived life, a blend of authenticity and resilience that transforms the lead of adversity into the gold of personal growth.

CHAPTER 14
MENTORSHIP AND COMMUNITY SERVICE: A WAY OF LIFE

What we do for ourselves dies with us. What we do for others and the world remains and is immortal.

– Albert Pike

From a young age, I embraced the philosophy of paying it forward—planting seeds in a garden I may never see bloom. Offering my time and energy generously is one of the most impactful gifts one can give. This approach wasn't merely about altruism; it became a vital part of my healing process, especially during some of the most challenging periods of my life.

Being present and forging meaningful relationships has been central to my personal growth. My commitment to truly listening has paid immense dividends, enriching my life with lessons from those I've mentored and, unexpectedly, from complete strangers. Their insights often arrived during my most vulnerable moments, ready to receive wisdom in its many forms. Even my children, with their fresh eyes and unfiltered perspectives, have been some of my greatest teachers.

Following the devastation of Hurricane Maria in Puerto Rico in 2017, I found myself grappling with the aftermath of death and destruction. This experience reopened unresolved emotions from years of similar deployments. The cumulative stress, combined with a painful divorce, pushed me to seek help. With the guidance of my therapist,

I navigated these dark times, identifying deep-seated issues and reinforcing the importance of professional mental health support.

This period of introspection reinforced my belief in the power of community. Being part of my church group and various men's groups provided not just a sense of belonging but also a mutual exchange of support and understanding. It is in these spaces that I have experienced therapy in its most organic form, offering and receiving care in a shared journey of healing.

Mentorship became a way for me to give back, to light a torch in the darkness and pay forward, sideways and backwards the kindness that had been shown to me. I established a filtering process to manage my time effectively, ensuring I could share my experiences without stretching myself too thin. This balance keeps me grounded, reminding me that there's only so much time in a day, and we must make the most of every moment we are given.

In my twenties, I made a conscious decision to live each day as if it were my last, setting daily goals to bring joy to others, often simply by sharing a smile. Amidst the pervasive negativity in the world, a smile has often served as a powerful counterforce, transforming the energy of an interaction or even a day. Early in life, I chose to move into neighborhoods and associate with people who didn't look like me. This decision, risky as it seemed, has enriched my life with diverse experiences and perspectives, fueling my growth and challenging me to adapt.

The tragic loss of my close friend and brother, Nathaneal Medrano, in July 1996, was a stark reminder of life's unpredictability. Nathaneal, a dedicated ATF agent, struggled with the consequences of a high-stakes case gone awry. Despite his commitment to influencing the final report, the burden became unbearable, leading to his tragic suicide. His death was a profound shock to all who knew him, serving as a painful lesson in the critical importance of mental wellness, especially in high-pressure jobs.

Nathaneal's story and the ripple effects of his life and death have profoundly impacted me. They serve as a somber reminder of the importance of mental health support and the need to continually advocate for those who struggle in silence.

Balancing life's highs and lows requires intention and mindfulness. I've learned to navigate these complexities by embracing both the joys and challenges that come my way. As I dance through life, I remain wary of imposters and superficial interactions that can distract from genuine connections. The guiding principle of "trust, but verify" has become central to my interactions.

Living intentionally means prioritizing mentorship, fostering community, and remaining adaptable to change. It means learning from every situation and being prepared for life's unexpected turns. By sharing these experiences, I hope to inspire others to live fully, cherish each moment, and pay forward, sideways and backwards the kindness they've received in their own unique ways.

Throughout my journey of service and mentorship, I've come to realize that life isn't a straight line; it's more like a winding river, filled with unexpected bends, challenges, and lessons learned along the way. Each setback, failure, and success has contributed to the person I am today. Looking back on my experiences, I understand that it's not just the big moments that matter—it's the small lessons that shape our journey and help us evolve into the people we were always meant to be.

CHAPTER 15
LESSONS LEARNED: THE BENDS AND TWEAKS ALONG THE WAY

Anyone who stops learning is old, whether at twenty or eighty. Anyone who keeps learning stays young.

– Henry Ford

My journey is a continuous learning process—each lesson adding depth and dimension to my personal growth. I actively seek these insights, continually implementing best practices to minimize repetition and maximize efficiency. This commitment to lifelong learning isn't just a personal philosophy; it's the compass guiding me through life's complexities. I adapt, I transform, I grow, recognizing that hardship and joy are universal experiences, shaping us all in profound ways.

The key is to integrate these lessons swiftly. Humans naturally resist change, but it's inevitable—a river constantly carving a new path. I've learned to become a proactive navigator, anticipating the bends in the river and preparing for the currents. The sooner we recognize change on the horizon, the sooner we can find our footing, and ultimately, those around us will benefit as well.

One significant bend in my river was the realization that I lacked strong male role models, particularly regarding fatherhood and marriage. Instead of passively accepting this void, I actively sought guidance. In retrospect, a simple book might have sufficed, but my path was a patchwork quilt of mentorship. I drew from various sources: family members, church leaders, mentors, and even friends. As men, we often complicate matters, allowing societal expectations and family pressures to dictate our paths. While foundational principles like the Golden Rule are essential, the definition of masculinity is far more nuanced than rigid societal definitions.

I'm deeply grateful for the men who stepped into my life, offering their wisdom and challenging me to break free from outdated molds. They helped me become a better person, husband, and father. Their influence shaped my understanding of manhood—not as a rigid set of rules, but as a journey of compassion, empathy, and personal growth. One mentor, a seasoned father, taught me the importance of active listening, not just hearing words, but truly understanding unspoken emotions. Another, a respected community leader, showed me the power of leading by example, demonstrating humility and service. These lessons, woven into the fabric of my life, became cornerstones of my own approach to fatherhood and marriage.

The lessons I've gathered aren't just for my benefit; they're meant to be shared. By actively seeking insights and embracing change, I've discovered not only personal growth but also a deeper understanding of the human experience. Becoming a better version of ourselves is a continuous journey, requiring self-reflection and a willingness to learn from every experience, whether joyous or painful. This ongoing evolution is the key to a more fulfilling life, one continuously shaped by lessons learned and a commitment to growth. The river continues to flow, and I continue to navigate its currents with intention and adaptability.

Chapter 16
ACCOMPLISHMENTS, CELEBRATION, RECOGNITION; DO IT!

People will forget what you said, people will forget what you did, but people will never forget how you made them feel.

– Maya Angelou

Acknowledgment and appreciation are fundamental human needs. Everyone, from the youngest child to the most seasoned professional, craves recognition—to feel valued and seen. It's not about ego; it's about the inherent human desire to know our contributions matter. Recognizing others strengthens relationships and fosters a positive environment, whether it's with our children, students, colleagues, or friends. Applying the art of "no", welcoming debate, exercising diplomacy, increasing knowledge and delegating to others are significant steps in balancing life.

Finding the Balance

However, celebrating achievements requires balance. While every team member deserves acknowledgment for their participation, not every effort warrants a trophy. In sports or the workplace, recognizing exceptional contributions encourages healthy competition and fuels growth. Just as a gardener selectively prunes a plant to encourage stronger growth, targeted recognition can inspire individuals to reach their full potential.

Lessons in Receiving and Giving

I learned the importance of celebrating both big and small wins later in life. My previous bosses often reminded me that while I readily celebrated others, I often overlooked my own accomplishments. This realization helped me appreciate the fist bumps, the pats on the back, and the verbal accolades that marked milestones in my journey. Celebrations and recognitions, whether written, verbal, or both, should be timely and sincere, reflecting both personal and professional growth.

Personal Lessons from Military Honors

My military service was punctuated by significant recognitions, including the Meritorious Service Medal, Coast Guard Commendation Medals, and the Navy and Marine Corps Achievement Medal. These awards weren't just for display; they affirmed my hard work, dedication, and sacrifices. One memorable moment was receiving the Meritorious Service Medal for leading a complex search and rescue operation during a raging storm. The weight of that medal wasn't just about the metal; it was the tangible representation of the team's collective effort and the lives we saved. This experience underscored the power of formal recognition to validate and motivate. It taught me that acknowledging contributions, both big and small, fuels a sense of purpose and inspires continued excellence.

The Personal Touch in Everyday Recognition

This understanding extends beyond formal awards. Sometimes, a simple gesture like bringing in coffee for the team after a challenging week speaks volumes. Other times, a handwritten note acknowledging a colleague's specific contribution can make their day. Learning to accept recognition graciously has also been a part of my growth. Humility is important, but allowing ourselves and others to enjoy well-earned praise is equally crucial.

Recognizing Others, Enriching Ourselves

In every sphere of life, we should celebrate—sometimes, simply for the sake of celebrating. These moments nurture spirits, build bonds, and remind us that our contributions, no matter how small, are valuable. As we navigate life's currents, let's remember the power of a simple "thank you" or a well-timed compliment. These acts of recognition are more than just pleasantries; they are profound expressions of respect and appreciation that can transform relationships and enrich our shared human experience. By acknowledging the light in others, we ignite our own.

Chapter 17
RELATIONSHIP, LIFE PARTNER, NEXT CHAPTER IN MOTION

Grow old along with me! The best is yet to be.
— Robert Browning

As I step into this pivotal chapter of life, I find myself drawn to the importance of genuine connection. I'm on a quest to find, or bump into, a life partner—a kindred spirit to share in the joys and challenges of life, someone aligned in values and dreams, with whom I can grow old. It's a journey that requires presence, energy, and a deep understanding of what truly matters: spirituality, family, community, and, above all, patience. Each encounter is an opportunity to apply the lessons I've learned, weaving a bond that resonates with the path I've carved.

Dating at this stage of life is both exhilarating and, at times, exhausting. Yet, it is a journey filled with possibility— a mosaic of experiences that offer glimpses of what could be. My travels have introduced me to diverse cultures and personalities, each a chance to learn and teach. To navigate these relationships, I've developed a personal roadmap, a filter guided by kindness and self-awareness. It's not about perfection but about finding that intangible feeling of "rightness," a connection that brings peace and joy.

Retirement: A New Chapter Unfolds

This chapter of my life isn't defined solely by personal relationships; it's also about embracing the broader adventure of retirement. Transitioning into "operation retirement mode" has been both a blessing and a unique challenge—one marked by the freedom to engage only in what truly ignites my passion. For decades, my life was defined by multiple phones ringing off the hook, constant demands for my attention, and the relentless pressures of staying 'in the know.' Now, I relish the simplicity of having just one phone number—a single connection to the world. This newfound simplicity has brought clarity, grounding me in what matters most.

In this phase, I am intentional about my time. I focus on learning, mentoring, spending quality moments with family and friends, and giving back to my community. Each day is an opportunity to contribute meaningfully, whether through volunteering, sharing wisdom, or simply being present for those who need a listening ear. It's a life of purpose, driven by the belief that joy is found in both the grand gestures and the quiet, everyday moments.

The Joy of Travel: Seeking Authenticity

Travel remains a cornerstone of my journey, a source of inspiration and growth. But it's not the typical tourist experience I crave. I steer away from the well-trodden paths, immersing myself in local life to experience the world as it truly is. Whether it's sharing a meal with strangers in a tucked-away village or learning the customs of a new culture, these authentic encounters bring me closer to the essence of humanity. They remind me that, no matter how different we appear on the surface, we all seek connection, understanding, and meaning.

Gratitude and Reflection

As I reflect on how far I've come, I am deeply grateful for the sacrifices of the past and the opportunities that lie ahead. This chapter is more than just a transition; it's a canvas for paying it forward. I've come to see life as a continuous flow of experiences, each day offering a chance to learn, connect, and contribute. Whether it's a moment of personal growth, mentoring someone in need, or simply placing a smile on a stranger's face, I am committed to living with intention and kindness.

In this season of life, gratitude is my compass. I cherish the privilege of time—time to explore, time to connect, and time to reflect. Each moment, no matter how small, is an opportunity to honor the lessons I've learned and to share them with others.

Embracing the Flow of Life

Standing at this crossroads, I am reminded that life is not a destination but a journey—a river that flows with endless opportunities, bends, and currents. With love on the horizon and retirement offering the freedom to chart my own course, I embrace this chapter with an open heart and a sense of possibility. It promises to be one of the most fulfilling yet, a testament to living authentically, intentionally, and with gratitude for every step along the way.

THE END

APPENDIX
SIGNIFICANT PROFESSIONAL ACHIEVEMENTS AND POSITIONS

U.S. Coast Guard Career

Officer & Enlisted Assignments Timeline:

- 2023-2024: LANTAREA CG-35 – Senior Reserve Officer & Branch Chief
- 2020-2023: Senior Defense Official; Defense Attaché (SDO/DATT), Port-Au-Prince, Haiti
- 2018-2020: Senior Reserve Officer, SEC Honolulu Command Cadre, Honolulu, HI
- 2015-2018: Emergency Preparedness Liaison Officer, District 11, Alameda, CA
- 2013-2015: Joint 35 Staff, U.S. Pacific Command, Honolulu, HI
- 2008-2012: Enforcement Duty & Response Management, Sector LA/LB, San Pedro, CA
- 2006-2007: Contingency Planner – Duty, Atlantic Area Contingency Plans Branch
- 2004-2006: Logistics Department Head & Assistant Operations Officer, Maritime Security Response Team, Chesapeake, VA
- 2003-2004: Operations Officer, MSST 91102 (transition to MSRT), Chesapeake, VA
- 2002-2004: Commandant Duty, Prevention & Response, Coast Guard HQ, Washington, DC

- 2000-2002: Harbor Defense Command 114, Long Beach, CA
- 1994-1999: Marine Safety Office/Group Los Angeles/Long Beach, San Pedro, CA
- 1990-1994: Boot Camp (Cape May, NJ) & Station Channel Islands, Port Hueneme, CA

Key Roles and Responsibilities:

- Played critical leadership roles in operational, logistical, safety, and contingency planning capacities throughout over 30 years of distinguished active duty and reserve service in the U.S. Coast Guard and Naval Coastal Warfare.
- Deployed globally with the U.S. Naval Coastal Warfare & Harbor Defense Command as the unit Intel officer, facility security officer, weapons officer, and force protection officer, responsible for the security and movement of equipment and personnel.
- Maintained and implemented contingency plans for homeland security, critical infrastructure protection, and continuity of operations.
- Supported National Special Security Event (NSSE) missions and partnered with U.S. federal agencies to enhance maritime safety and security.

Entertainment Industry

- Actor (SAG-AFTRA): Lead, principal, and featured roles in numerous television shows, films, and commercials.
- Technical Advisor: Provided military, law enforcement, and business consultation to directors and producers on various projects.
- Producer: Led or assisted in the production of several film and television projects.
- Instructor: Motorcycle rider courses for new and experienced riders.

Education and Training

- Adjunct Professor: Instructed Counter-Terrorism and Intelligence courses for security, fire, military, police, and federal personnel.

Consulting and Advisory Roles

- Consultant: Provided business strategy and process improvement consulting to various companies and boards.
- Security Consultant: Conducted security assessments, surveys, and provided high-end event or dignitary protection services for various clients.

Corporate Leadership Roles

Pinkerton Government Services, Inc. and Consulting Services; Vice President, Global Account Manager, and Senior Consultant:

- Provided strategic direction, leadership, and management across 35 sites with over 800 team members, managing the Global Boeing Company Contract.
- Ensured short- and long-term revenue growth and profitability objectives were met while managing an operational budget of $40 million and identifying growth opportunities with the business development staff.
- Delivered high-quality, proactive customer service; evaluated service quality, measured, reviewed, and reported performance metrics. Initiated corrective actions as necessary.
- Led, directed, planned, and oversaw company-wide physical security programs and initiatives, providing threat, labor dispute, and contract management solutions.
- Maintained clearances as one of the FSOs/Investigators and performed audits, implementing best practices and promoting team member training and development.
- Ensured compliance with applicable laws, standards, regulations, policies, and procedures

while resolving operational, legal, financial, or administrative issues.

- Actively participated in national policy review and armed training committees, leading a team to complete complex risk, safety, executive protection, and security assessments/investigations with actionable recommendations.

Director of Safety, Security & Environmental Compliance, Nautilus International (Metro Ports/Metro Cruise/Metro Shore):

- Led and oversaw high-performing safety, security, and environmental programs. Coordinated complex tasks encompassing cybersecurity in the maritime domain.
- Oversaw risk management and insurance policies, ensuring compliance with federal, state, and local safety rules and regulations.
- Conducted safety, security, and compliance inspections and surveyed occupational conditions of vessel operations and terminal facilities.
- Maintained a culture of continuous improvement in corporate safety through leadership and training and interfaced with various agencies overseeing workplace safety.

Valley Economic Development Corporation (VEDC); Board of Directors and Audit Committee Member (Non-Profit):

- Advised and governed the adherence to policies of a $30 million non-profit organization, providing counsel to leadership and promoting financial and loan services to support organizational goals.
- Reviewed financial audits and collaborated with CPA and auditing firms. Provided leadership for marketing, fundraising, and outreach events, while training the organizational management team.

About the Author

Greg Duncan's life reads like a Hollywood screenplay, filled with groundbreaking milestones and profound dedication. From becoming the first African American Coast Guard officer to complete the U.S. Naval elite scuba diving course to serving as a U.S. Diplomat in Haiti, his military exploits are nothing short of cinematic.

His prowess isn't confined to the military; Greg also navigated the vast challenges of the corporate world, spearheading security strategies for Boeing. Never one to shy away from new horizons, he embraced the arts as a credited SAG-AFTRA actor and producer, showcasing his versatility and relentless pursuit of new challenges.

Beyond his professional life, Greg is deeply devoted to community service and mentorship, actively participating in roles with Kappa Alpha Psi Fraternity Inc. and the SAG-AFTRA Military Veterans committee. His narrative continues to evolve as he steps into the world of literary arts as an author, ready to share his compelling story with the world.

Greg's journey is also one of personal joy and fulfillment, as a father to three awesome young adults. Residing in Southern California, maintaining a presence in Washington, D.C., and frequently visiting the Caribbean, he balances his dynamic career with a vibrant family life. Together, these threads weave a rich tapestry, capturing the essence of a truly remarkable life that inspires others to dream big and break barriers.

Aknowledgements

I want to personally thank each of you for your time, effort, creativity, talent, support and collaboration you gave me during this journey.

Sharon Duncan
Megan Duncan
Hailey Duncan
Kyle Duncan
Reggie Burton
Jon Huertas
Michael Bennett
Hayden Bone
Segaro Bozart

I wish you all the very best life offers, peace, good energy, good health, prosperity, happiness and absolute achievement in all your endeavors.

Respectfully,
Greg

www.ingramcontent.com/pod-product-compliance
Lightning Source LLC
LaVergne TN
LVHW020430070526
838199LV00025B/589/J